A NEW ORLEANS VOODOO
HERITAGE EDITION

TALKING TO GOD WITH FOOD
QUESTIONING ANIMAL SACRIFICE

ORDER OF SERVICE
SECOND IN A SERIES OF TEACHINGS

DR. LOUIE MARTINIÉ

BLACK MOON PUBLISHING
CINCINNATI, OHIO USA

Black Moon Manifesto

*It is the Will and mission of Bate Cabal/Black Moon to
effectively manifest unique and insightful occult Works
for the esoteric community in a manner that is unfettered
by commercial considerations.*

BlackMoonPublishing.com

Design and layout by
Joe Bounds of Black Moon Publishing

Cover photo:
Expedition to seek visions from the insect loa in response to
receiving their signature. Red palm oil and rice as offerings.

Photo by Mishlen Linden

Photo of Dr. Louie Martinié on back page
by Mishlen Linden

ISBN: 978-1-890399-72-6

United States • United Kingdom • Europe • Australia • India

Dedication

To all of the Kind Mothers of the past, the present, and the future. May your sufferings and pleasures find a voice in this writing.

Thanks

To Louis for his at times grudging dedication to the Work. To jo whose exquisitely dark esthetic is Black Moon. To Mishlen for inspiration and the all night sessions of art and writing. To Maegdlyn whose voice I now in radiance hear. To Priestess Miriam for the ever present blessings of her kind heart. To Mr. Norbu for his patience and continued presence.

To the readers and all those who have offered advice; with special thanks to Rekmel, Saresa, Nola, Nema, Dr. Marty Laubach, Rev. Severina K. M. Singh.

The New Orleans Voodoo Tarot was a work of love, knowledge, and understanding. My thoughts on sacrifice have developed with time and practice; I hope this writing adds a bit more wisdom to the gumbo.

CONTENTS

PROLOGUE

April, 6, 2002 — Too damn cold out for April. Not the weather for travel. I have a jacket in my hand and more than a bit of frost on my heart. I come into the Temple in Baton Rouge and find the Priestess speaking to a six year old girl. Jon, her assistant, is standing over by the ancestor altar. He is just back from a tour of Japan with his band.

Priestess asks, "Do you recognize her?" I draw a blank.

"You played for her baptism five years ago." I smile and my Spirits warm.

A little later Priestess, the girl, and her large family walk out to the street. They are going to the capital building to take in a bit of Huey P. Long and other state history.

"That girls a trip," Jon said. "When she first came in, she asked where Priestess was." She said, "Is she talking to God with food? That was a big cake last time"

The regular use of edible offerings is a feature that distinguishes New Orleans Voodoo from its Baptist and Catholic counterparts. The offering can be as simple as an apple, a dash of hot sauce, or as complex as an eight course meal. What is important is to realize that we believe the spirits require substance just as you and I require substance. This nourishment can take many forms; mineral, vegetable, or animal.

Three Questions

I want to begin to explore a subject of importance to all who wish to enter the world of New Orleans Voodoo. What I have to say is also applicable to anyone who follows a set of religious practices that include sacrifice, particularly the sacrifice of animals. New Orleans Voodoo is similar to African Voodoo, Haitian Voodoo, and to Santeria in embracing sacrifice, animal and other, in its ceremonies, initiations and confirmations.

Most people who are interested in Voodoo have some factual or fictional information regarding animal sacrifice and want to know more. They often want to ask about sacrifice but do not out of courtesy or from a fear of giving offense. They may be disturbed by the idea or it may hold an attraction for them due to its relatively exotic, forbidden nature. My goal is to begin to create a framework that makes it possible for the practitioner to approach the issue of animal sacrifice on the secure footing of systematic thought coupled with deep feeling; hopefully avoiding the slippery and sensationalistic aversion or attraction too often associated with the subject.

In the matter of animal sacrifice, you will likely be impelled by circumstance to make decisions at an early point in your road to the loa. There is no tower, ivy or otherwise, in which to sit and consider the issue of animal sacrifice at length once the process of initiation or confirmation has begun. The tide swells and you will be borne along by a combination of interest, time spent, love for the loa, money already committed, and a respect for your Temple and its clergy. Your course may then seem to be inalterably set in the direction of engaging in or abstaining from animal sacrifice. That is the case if choices are not made before your practice takes on such an impelling urgency.

At least three questions are necessary and legitimate to ask from the very beginning of your practice. The first question is best not only put to yourself but also to more experienced and knowledgeable voodoosants in the Temple of your choice. The latter two questions can only be answered by you in the most profound part of your being, the part that will eventually hold communion with the loa.

1. "Is it necessary to sacrifice animals in order to conduct an initiation or other ceremony to the loa?"

2. "Will I participate in ceremonies in which animals are sacrificed?"

3. "Will I myself sacrifice animals?"

Initiations may contain the sacrifice of an animal or animals. The costs of the animals are often cited as a part of the cost of the initiation. Initiation literally means "beginning," so the above questions must be asked and answered to your own satisfaction as early as possible. To postpone a choice frequently means that momentum rather than consideration makes the choice for you.

It is best if animal sacrifice is discussed with the clergy of your Temple as soon as it is proper and respectful for you to do so. This would be, as a rule of thumb, around the third meeting. The first of the three questions is a good way to broach this possibly sensitive topic. Initiation, its meaning and method, is a proper subject of inquiry. Your choices are best communicated to and discussed with the clergy of the particular Voodoo Temple with which you are in contact. The sooner this is done without self-righteousness or self-abnegation, the better. Perhaps it is wise to set apart a day of retreat to consider these questions. Remember that there are numerous Voodoo Temples and an abundance of methods to call the loa. Be both patient and persistent. The loa live in a realm very close to ours. They hear and what you need will come.

I believe that these three questions must be addressed equally with both the heart and the head. The head has the ability to weigh perspectives and facts from both sides of a question. What's more, the head contains the mouth and it is primarily by the mouth that we share what we know and gain knowledge. The heart, once it is brought into action, gives the answers a depth of understanding that provides an unshakable basis for the knowing. The sharing of understanding and knowledge is the very essence of our teaching in Voodoo. Be informed, be sensitive, and choose to the best of your ability. Actions, initial or otherwise, carry great weight but remember also that, with the growth of wisdom, choices and the actions that flow from those choices may be set on another course.

I do not know what your answer will be to the above three questions. I have no right to know outside of the formal relationship we could enter into within the context of a Voodoo Temple. I know the choices I have made and what these choices have brought me. That is enough; undue curiosity on the part of the teacher or student is a sign of deep disrespect.

While the above words on curiosity are true, it must also be acknowledged that there is a slant in all writings. The slant may be large or small and it may influence the reader in ways either subtle or gross. I am afraid that my slant against animal sacrifice is both large and gross. Not the best of combinations but in order to write with both my heart and head I must write from my perceptions and perspective.

My serious practice in Voodoo spans over thirty years. About ten years ago my choices in animal sacrifice were greatly influenced by conversations and contact with Tibetan Tantric elders. The elders of any of the religious traditions are each a global treasure. During the last few decades, there has been the increased opportunity for contact with Tibetan elders.

Their words have caused me to reexamine not so much my love for the loa as the ways in which that love is expressed. Their words have helped me to develop ways that bring more benefit to the loa and to myself. I believe that I now have more wisdom in discerning my position and the loas position relative to the whole of the spiritual universe.

My desire is that your choice be based on your own deep deliberations, relatively free from both covert and overt influence. When the slant of a piece of writing is known, the reader can better compensate for its influence. Therefore I will begin by communicating the choices I have made in response to these three questions. I do not make animal sacrifice and I do not participate in rites in which animals are sacrificed. I use Red Palm Oil with great success in rites both conformational and otherwise when animal sacrifice is traditionally indicated.

This is my slant and once forewarned I am sure that the reader can better compensate for the rather pervasive influence it exerts in these writings. Check all that I write. Think; deeply contemplate actions and their alternatives and the fruit that they bear. Choose freely and wisely. Choice stands at the wheel in navigating this river of the soul. There is no condemnation or commendation, only an ever-present responsibility that is built into the very fabric of the universe. We can choose in our actions; there is no choose involved in the consequences that they, by their nature, call

forth.

What I wish to do is to provide a framework that can be used by the new and the more experienced practitioner to examine or reexamine the position they choose to take in relation to animal sacrifice. The earlier parts of the book detail a larger context in which to place any of the practices involving giving something to the loa, spirits, or deities. Spiritual cause and effect and scapegoating are examined in the mid sections. The ending section compares western medical practices and voodoo practices as they relate to the use of animals in formulating cures. In conclusion, a table clarifying forms and functions of giving and a listing of objects and actions that may be given to individual loa is appended.

From Gift to Sacrifice

GIFT: "to give" [OE <gifan "to give"]

PRESENT: "to exhibit" "to be before" [< OF presenter < L praesentare "to exhibit" < praeesse < prae - before" + esse "to be"]

OFFERING: "to bring before" [< OE offrian "to offer, esp. a sacrifice," ult. < L offer "to present" < ob - before + ferre "to bring"]

SACRIFICE: "to make sacred" [<. L. sacrificium; sacer sacred + facere to make.] (All above from Webster's Revised Unabridged Dictionary, © 1996, 1998 MICRA, Inc.).

It is useful for the sake of this writing to distinguish between gifts, presents, offerings, and sacrifices. These words and the actions they refer to serve to create a cascade of meaning that seizes and places animal sacrifice within a clear and understandable context. I will rely heavily on the roots or origins of these words to clarify their differences and similarities. The roots of words have been described as "language's unconscious." (Bob Contradino conversation; 1984). It is perhaps in this "unconscious" that the ancient creation of similarity and difference exists in its most primary sense.

Gift: "to give"

Here there is a simple outward flow. There is an expansiveness in the act of giving that defies the logic of reciprocity. Pure giving seeks nothing in return. The self is forgotten in favor of the other. There is no expectation, denotation, or connotation of something coming back to the giver of the gift. Recompense is not in the equation. There is simply an outward flowing from the giver to the receiver.

It is logically nonsensical, though sometimes socially proper, to speak of paying back a gift. This would not be a gift so much as a "transaction," often in the sense of a business "transaction." Perhaps the false refinement of "gift" is preferred by some to the more realistic coarseness of "transaction."

The function of a gift is very specific. Gifts can create the ability or occasion to respond but in no way the mandate, obligation, or expectation to respond. A gift given to the loa purely creates a pathway along which relationship can flow.

"Give me," "bring me," "heal me," or "open for me" all have their place in our communication with the loa. They are honorable subtexts in which to conduct this

communication but they are not proper in the larger context of "gift." Gifts are rare, seldom offered in New Orleans Voodoo or in life in general. It is my experience that gifts are most often offered to the Master of the Head. The bond and love between you and the loa who is the Master of your Head is usually so great that the giving of gifts flows naturally. Also, the Awakened Beings or Buddhas of the Tibetan Tantrics are said to want or require nothing from us. All the benefit we can receive from them is a pure gift.

Elegant in their simplicity, "I give to you" are the first and final words of gift giving.

Present:
"to exhibit before", "to be before"

A present is freely given to the loa. As with a gift, a present carries no sense of reciprocity. It is given and nothing is expected in return. The difference between a gift and a present is that a gift is usually an object and a present, while it can be an object, can also consist of a more subtle type of giving.

To present oneself to the loa fully in the present is perhaps the best present you can offer to them or, for that matter, to any other sentient being. To give what you are doing right now on an ongoing basis is a marvelous "present of the present." These little plays on words communicate a great mysterie in a hopefully

more amusing than irritating manner.

In this mysterie is contained an essential quality of spiritual love. Through our attention and its focus everything we do can become a great present. Our attention and its focusing, the active and willful directing of this attention, is itself a sacred act. So often we move like sleep-walkers and our attention is not so much focused as leaked out upon the world. Focus is forgotten in this bottomless sleep. We all too often look without seeing, touch without feeling, and know without understanding. This is a tragedy in that so much is available to our focused attention and so little is this attention used. Suffering easily manifests in this type of neglectful sleep.

Our attention, when focused in the present moment, is actually all that we can call our own. It is the only thing that we truly possess. The past, the future, the fleeting firework like displays of our senses that rush into the vastness of space and time lie beyond the boundaries of our reach. They can only be affected indirectly. Our attention and its play in the moment is our sole province.

To give the present moment in its fullness via our attention to whomever or whatever we are with is very difficult due to the rapidly changing patterns of the mind. It is only through diligent practice that the ability to focus the attention for any amount of time appears. The loa or any other recipient of this full attention receives a nurturing shower of manna. Their very being, exactly as it exists, is affirmed in the gift of this focused attention. They are recognized; they have a witness to their being and becoming. We hear the very Word of their Soul.

In addition, it is good to consider that any thought of return or benefit pulls us out of the present moment and into a smaller world whose narrow measure is closely taken by some future gain and loss.

Offering:
"to bring before"

To make an offering is to "bring something before" a spirit, loa, or deity. The something that is brought falls into two categories.

The practitioner brings an:

(1) action, or an
(2) object.

The practitioner then transfers what is brought to a spirit, loa, or deity with conscious thought of or concern for receiving something in return. Within the context of this book, an offering does not include the death or suffering of a living being. Spiritual practices in which a being dies or suffers are known as "sacrifice" and will be examined in detail later in this book.

Many dictionaries use "sacrifice" and "offering" interchangeably. I believe that there is a subtle and valuable connotative if not denotative difference between the two words. If I tell you that I am going to the Temple to make an offering, perhaps fruit, wheat, or perfume comes to mind. If I say that I am going to make a sacrifice, most people would take this to mean that I am going to take the life of or offer flesh or the organs from some creature. My experience is that this distinction holds for New Orleans Voodoo. Offerings do not contain the suffering of animals. This section concerns itself with offerings of objects or actions.

An offering is not a gift or a present; giving and receiving both carry weight in an offering. Receiving is now part of our equation. In a sense, an offering is a payment for some benefit we have received or hope to receive. Offerings always carry the implication that something will come back to us in return. The favor of the loa, the fulfillment of a need, the fanning of a desire, a healing of the body or soul are some of the rewards for making offerings. In making offerings to the loa there is always some sense of exchange, the loa are given something that they need or desire in exchange for their help in obtaining something that we need or desire. While offerings are not infused with the nobility that lies in the openhandedness of a gift or a present, the making of offerings is certainly an honorable and respectful way to communicate with the loa.

Offerings are used in most religions, faiths, and

systems of spiritual practice. They forge a strong reciprocal link between the person making the offering and the loa, spirit, deity, or God/dess to whom the offering is made. Money is an offering much favored by Christian religions. In the Roman Catholic mass there is a time set aside for the collection of monetary offerings from the congregation. The Christian evangelists who people the landscape of televised visions frequently ask for offerings of money. Offerings to the Christian Saint Jude often carry the proviso, "I will give you____if you____."

Buddhists give flowers, money, food, and specially constructed statues to an array of protective deities who act to preserve the teachings of Buddhism. The Buddhas themselves want or need nothing but our welfare. Their motivation is only to bring us happiness and to help relieve our suffering. In terms of our definitions, the Buddhas are most properly given gifts or presents, not offerings.

Wicca and other pagan and neo-pagan religions make offerings to the elemental spirits of the earth, air, fire, and water and to deities such as Aradia. Offerings can also be made to a variety of ancient deities. For example, Venus / Aphrodite can be offered flowers or sweet foods in order to bring love to the petitioner. New Orleans Spiritual Churches make offerings to the spirits, for example to the great Native American spirit Black Hawk, in exchange for help and protection.

A contribution is a type of offering. This is true

for political parties as well as for churches and temples. Special consideration by politicians as they decide economic issues as well as special seating in a church or temple can both be dependent on the size of contributions.

This serves to introduce an important consideration in the making of offerings. There is usually a correspondence between the amount offered and the amount of benefit received in return for the offering. Large offerings bring large benefit. It is important for us to remember that the loa appreciate that what is large for one individual may be small for another. In my experience, the loa are not so much bookkeepers, comparing neat columns of figures, as keepers of the heart's much less exact but more accurate reckonings.

Sacrifice:
"to make sacred"

January 5th 2001 — Offering to Mama Waters; Gulf of Mar Assai on the Island of Saint Rose.

Honor and Respect to Mama Waters. Offered Sweet wheat to the salt winds, the sand, and to the Great Waters. I now have a deep sense of being welcomed to this sea.

At first I was going to give Mama Waters some of the meat from a sandwich I had with me, but then I thought of Mama as the mother of all life. You don't offer a mother the flesh of one of her dead children.

Decided on an offering instead of a sacrifice.

A sacrifice is not the same as an offering. All sacrifices, as the word is used in this writing, include in some way the death or suffering of a sentient being. Offerings consist of objects or actions and as such are not sacrifices. The essential quality of a sacrifice is that the life form sacrificed is a sentient being. Sentient beings are beings with senses. They have some type of hearing, sight, touch, taste, smell, or sense of movement; they use one or all of these senses to know their world, to seek happiness and to avoid suffering. Sentience points to the presence of consciousness, which can be defined as the ability to interpret the information received from those senses and to move toward happiness (pleasure) and away from suffering (undesired pain).

The making of a sacrifice involves the death or suffering of a sentient being. This sentence is a bit jarring in its stark simplicity. Some being that was living will be dead or suffering after the completion of a sacrifice. The beings life / flesh / blood are sacrificed to a spirit, deity, God/dess or, in the context of New Orleans Voodoo, to a loa. The loa take nourishment from the life-force contained in the flesh, blood and fluids of the sacrificed creature. For this nourishment to be available, the being that is sacrificed must suffer or die.

To make a sacrifice is to "make sacred." The life form is "made sacred" in being sacrificed to a higher

power. The belief is that the beings small life is made larger, through that life being given to a greater, more powerful being. According to this line of thought, all involved benefit when a sacrifice is offered.

Sacrifice is not an idea or practice that is foreign to western culture. It is good to remember that the derivation of "blessed" is "blooded" or "originally probably to consecrate by sprinkling with blood (Webster's Revised Unabridged Dictionary, © 1996, 1998 MICRA, Inc.)." Blood sacrifice is a concept based upon a practice firmly entrenched in the language of western culture. It is certainly not a practice imported from Asia, Africa or from anywhere else. It is a part of every westerner's heritage.

"A holy priesthood to offer up spiritual sacrifices." (1 Pet. ii. 5)

"Offering an oblation, dedicated to God. Thus Cain consecrated to God of the first-fruits of the earth, and Abel of the firstlings of the flock" (Gen. 4:3,4). -(Source: Easton's 1897 Bible Dictionary)

Sacrifice is no foreign or exotic encroachment on the Western cultural terrain. The story of Cain and Able enjoys a high level of popular recognition and it is Able, the good brother, who sacrifices.

In the giving of a sacrifice with intent of benefit, there is a responsibility created on the part of the spirit, loa, or deity that receives the sacrifice. Reciprocity is affirmed and the practitioner can effectively ask for something. Money, less harassment at work, a better job, luck in love, and the return of an unfaithful loved one are all desires that can be brought to fruition through sacrifice.

This raises two important questions. The first being, "Is there another less drastic way to get these desires?" Sacrifice involves the death or suffering of a sentient being. Such death or suffering is an extreme means to gain the end desired. Is there a less extreme means available? I remember being with Priest Oswan of the New Orleans Voodoo Spiritual Temple when a client asked him to work a spell so that he could win the love of a woman. Oswan looked him in the eye and said, "Did you ever try courting her? You have spent a lot of time in here. If you had spent that time with her, she might love you now." Here Priest Oswan's wise advice was to move beyond preconceptions of what was necessary to obtain a given end and choose the simplest path possible.

"Is what I want worth the death or suffering of a sentient being?" is the second, very personal question. To answer this question you must decide if sentient life has a value to you in and of itself. If you believe that life is special or sacred in itself, then the reason to stop or disrupt a life must be more special or more sacred than that life. Perhaps a better job is not worth the death or suffering of a sentient being; perhaps it is.

Sentience and intelligence are two related but very different characteristics of organisms. General western culture has voiced some concern about the taking of intelligent life but not the taking of sentient life. The relative concern for the welfare of dolphins is an example of this. The more intelligence dolphins are shown to have, the more concern there is about their killing. Intellect is valued over and above all other means of knowing the world. Fish are fair game while dolphins are not. Both are sentient creatures of the ocean. Both suffer when killed. I have seen fear in the eyes of a fish as it suffocated. I have seen suffering in its movements. But the suffering of the dolphin is somehow more meaningful, more important because of its higher intelligence.

I believe that this is the attitude of the conquistadors, and of all other imperialists and colonialists; "To be respected, you must be as I see myself." We see ourselves as possessing an intelligence that serves to differentiate us from the rest of the natural world, therefore any other life form thought to possess a degree of such intelligence is deserving of special respect and treatment. The elder Tibetans teach that it is not intelligence so much as sentience that matters. The Tibetan view greatly expands the context in which life is valued. I have found this respect for all sentient beings rather than just intelligent beings to be instrumental in working with the insect loa. These loa are certainly sentient though not what we would call intelligent. If I killed their brothers and sisters in the Visible World, the great insect loa would certainly not have ridden (possessed) and taught me.

The following list examines a number of affirmations and objections to sacrifice in a point by point manner. In general, pro positions are followed by con positions. Again, as I explained at the beginning of this teaching, I now have a bias toward not giving sentient beings in sacrifice. This bias may give an added weight to the con side. For this I apologize.

PRO: Sacrifice makes sacred the life of the being that is sacrificed.
CON: All life is sacred in and of itself. Sacrifice is not necessary to make it sacred.

PRO: Sacrifice makes the being that is sacrificed spiritually larger.
CON: A small fish does not become greater by being eaten by a bigger fish. We grow spiritually through our own efforts.

PRO: The being that is sacrificed is absorbed and made a part of the larger spirit, loa, or deity to which it is sacrificed. It offers a quick means to spiritual growth.
CON: This assumes that one life form can absorb another life form. We may remain individuals forever or until the universe goes away. Also, there is no way to assure that the being wants to become a part of a larger entity.

PRO: The being will be better treated if raised and

sacrificed in a temple than if raised and killed in a factory for use in the food industry.

CON: True; but neither a temple nor the factory is acceptable. One does not justify the other. You were physically better treated as a house slave than as a field slave. The existence of field slaves does not justify the existence of house slaves.

PRO: The offering of bloody sacrifice is an important part of both the Western and the African heritage.

CON: While this is true it is also irrelevant and it justifies nothing. The taking of human beings as slaves is also a part of these heritages. Massacres of innocents and the rules or cruel tyrants are important parts of these heritages. Few would want to follow these practices now.

PRO: We all die at some time; this is the best way to die.

CON: Perhaps it is simply an unnecessary way to die if life is sacred to begin with.

PRO: It saves the lives of human beings (this is examined in a following section on medicine and healing).

CON: The taking of life may be too high a price to pay for the saving of your own life or the life of another.

PRO: When the sacrifice is performed the priest or priestess may be possessed by one of the loa. It is not his or her hand that wields the knife. (The Oguns, in

that they are iron are the usual loa for this).
CON: There is a chain of cause and effect that is initiated by the priest or priestess. They began the series of actions and therefore carry the responsibility for the sacrifice that is its outcome.

PRO: The loa need the sacrifice to survive.
CON: The loa grow and evolve as we grow and evolve. As they have not kept the same form in the millennia since their inception in Africa, so they do not have the same needs and appetites.

What is and what is not a sacrifice is not as simple a question as it appears. Much depends on our beliefs about the abilities of other life forms. The presence or absence of life is fairly easy to discern but whether that life has some kind of sensory derived knowledge of the world is another matter. In the end, it may be a matter of belief. If you believe that plants such as sage or sweetgrass have consciousness, that they are in some manner sentient, have some sort of senses, react with pain or pleasure; then if you offer them in a ritual it is a sacrifice. If you believe that a fish is sentient, then the offering of a fish is a sacrifice. It may be useful to list life forms ranging from microbes to plants to trees to insects to reptiles to mammals and so forth, and then to consider if their being offered in a rite would be a sacrifice and if it is your will to be a part of such a rite.

Animal Sacrifice

Winter, 1982 - I've been at the little storefront on Claiborne for three hours. The old conjure woman sat amid piles of colorful fabric punctuated by alters brightly crowned with saint candles. She sewed and I sat. The questions I had asked were serious and she had motioned me to wait. Now I understood that it was my job to sit quietly, and to come again and again if necessary. I was the one asking, it was her call whether to answer or not.

The steady movements of the needle stopped and she looked up at me.

"You showed respect by waitin. I don't have to talk if it's not in me. Now I feel like it."

Her eyes narrowed as she looked at me.

"Do you know how many animals have to die to make an initiation?" She shook her head. She began a list of animals. A barnyard full. Her voice sounded a little sad, a little disgusted.

She ended by telling me to always keep a penny in my shoe. If the penny turned colors I'd know that someone was working against me.

Putting the issue of intelligence aside, there is a general agreement that animals are sentient beings.

They use their senses to know the world and to seek pleasure and happiness and to avoid pain and suffering. Not all sentient beings are animals. Most people would say that a fish is also sentient. A few less would say that a reptile is sentient. Even less would call an insect sentient and fewer still would grace a plant with sentience. Still, some people would grant sentience to all of the above life forms.

We are well equipped at this point in our journey to look at the subject of animal sacrifice. We have a context that moves from gift to present to offering to sacrifice and have met the issue of sentience. My first thought in writing was to simply call this chapter "Sacrifice" but my experience is that many people drawn to Voodoo will be faced with the specific question of animal sacrifice. Precision is necessary in as charged a subject as animal sacrifice and I believe that this precision is best applied in the development of a vocabulary to effectively discuss and think about this subject.

Animal sacrifice is not an offering. It is a type of sacrifice; the sacrifice of an animal. If you believe that fish, reptiles, birds, insects, trees, and plants are sentient, then to offer any of these would be a sacrifice but not an animal sacrifice. My point is that animal sacrifice occupies a relatively small portion of the map that depicts our dealings with the loa. Necessary or not, it is a small portion. The loa can be fed and honored in many other ways. And, possibly, alternatives to animal sacrifice can be found.

The question is not if animal sacrifice is effective. Yes, it is effective in bringing certain types of benefit. The question here is if animal sacrifice is *necessary*. Atomics may effectively clear the enemy from a battlefield but may not be necessary and may in the end be detrimental to all involved. The analogy to atomics is a good one. Animal sacrifice will get the job done in the short term. But when considering long term spiritual development, it may be detrimental to the practitioner. It may leave a type of "fallout" that slowly poisons the soul. Perhaps, when examined on a case by case basis, an offering could serve both us and the loa just as well.

Other faiths and religions have at some point in their history contained rites involving the sacrifice of animals. The early Christians offered blood sacrifice. All religions and faiths evolve. The movement toward bloodless offerings seems to be a part of this evolution. The tastes of the loa change along with the appearance that they assume and the rites to which they respond. Possibly New Orleans Voodoo is following the course of other faiths and religions by moving toward giving the loa mange sec (dry or bloodless meals) rather than meals that are mange rouge (red or bloody meals). The tastes of the loa themselves seem to be changing.

Scapegoats

Thou shalt offer every day a bullock for a sin offering for atonement. —Ex. xxix. 36.

In New Orleans Voodoo, to scapegoat is to transfer unwanted elements, be they sins, faults, or diseases of the body or spirit, to another sentient being. The life of the sentient being is then terminated in a rite similar to sacrifice and the body as a container of the transferred faults is returned to the earth to be cleansed. Scapegoating is similar to sacrifice in that a sentient being is killed but that being is not "made sacred." It is made the opposite of sacred, or "unclean" by the transfer of sins or diseases.

Christians who practice scapegoating in the context of New Orleans Voodoo face a particularly poignant situation. To the Christian, Christ is the archetypal scapegoat. He suffered and died to redeem all from their sins. He took our sins upon Himself and was sacrificed on the cross. He willingly took the sins of the entire planet upon Himself.

For the Christian there is an awe-inspiring equivalency here. If the Christian uses the practice of scapegoating, then the scapegoat stands in the place of Christ and the practitioner stands in the place of those who took the life of Christ. The implications of this for the Christian practitioner of scapegoating in New Orleans Voodoo are potentially monstrous.

Buddhists hold that each sentient life has an intrinsic value. Due to reincarnation, an animal could have been a man or woman in a past incarnation. It is only at this moment in time that the being is an animal. Additionally, it would be a useless act for a Buddhist to attempt to transfer personal suffering to another being. The karma of such a transfer would catch up with the practitioner in this life or the next probably as a multiple of the original suffering. Scapegoating would be a jump from the proverbial frying pan into the fire. The personal suffering of the present would be multiplied in the future.

A symbol is something that stands for something else and the scapegoat as a form of sacrifice is a symbol carried to the extreme. The scapegoat is a stand in for the person who suffers from a physical or spiritual ailment. The scapegoat "stands in" and takes the ailment from the person and is then sacrificed. This sounds a bit particular and exotic, but nothing could be further from the truth. Western culture is rife with scapegoating. It is a prerogative of the powerful. If a rich man and a poor man are accused of a crime and arraigned together in a western court, it does not take much imagination to predict who will probably get the lighter sentence and who will take the full brunt of the fall. Big business is rampant with scapegoating. If a problem arises, inferiors are expected to take the blame, leaving the hands of the boss clean. The lower class historically becomes the scapegoat of the upper class.

Scapegoating as practiced in New Orleans Voodoo does work but the price may be exceptionally high. To benefit directly from the pain of another, particularly if the other is relatively unable to defend themselves, is a corruption of one's basic humanity. It is without honor. Our humanity makes possible an appreciation of connectedness with all other life forms. Scapegoating denies this connection. Scapegoating is a practice of the exploiters brought into the Temple.

Consent and Sacrifice

In a many rites of sacrifice, the being to be sacrificed is asked to give consent. This consent is necessary for the rite to be performed. Without this consent, the life force of the being would not be able to be transferred to the spirit, loa, God/dess receiving the sacrifice. The road would be blocked by the beings resistance.

Such consent is extremely difficult to verify. Traditionally food is placed before the being to be sacrificed. The food is sometimes placed within a ritual diagram such as a veve. If the being takes the food, this is interpreted as agreement to the sacrifice. For example, corn can be placed before a chicken in a veve and if the chicken takes the corn the action is interpreted as consent to be sacrificed. A chicken pecking at corn or an animal taking food placed before it is a common enough action. To interpret such an action even in ritual context as agreement to be sacrificed is questionable.

There is no intrinsic connection between eating the food and giving consent to be sacrificed. Using the same line of thought, I could prepare a buffet for a Mardi Gras banquet, place the alcohol within certain diagrams, and then say that those who took a drink had acquiesced to be sacrificed. This is obviously not the case. I would only have to ask the drinkers their opinion on the subject. Mardi Gras is a highly improper time for any kind of sacrifice. There is plenty of time in Lent for that sort of thing if the drinkers so wished.

The problem is that the chicken and most other animals have problems using Creole, Standard English, French or whatever language is being spoken in the rite. Consent is always, to some degree, a matter of interpretation. This is a tremendous burden on the practitioner doing the interpreting and on those participating in the ceremony. In such an important matter, all must be completely satisfied that consent has been given. I would personally be more comfortable if the being were to scratch a word in the dirt to give consent.

Slavery and Sacrifice

TC, a practitioner and friend, points out that what is sacrificed is thought of as belonging to the person making the sacrifice. I am amazed by the powerful simplicity of this statement. It is possible to own an offering consisting of an object or an action. The object or the action is yours to give; it has no will of its own.

A sacrifice involves another sentient being, not an object or action that can be owned. TC's words raised an important question. Can a practitioner own another sentient being so completely that he or she can sacrifice that being? I cannot sacrifice something that I do not consider in some way mine and I do not believe that it is possible to own another sentient being. If I do not "own" what I am "giving," there can be no or only incidental benefit to me.

Other sentient beings can be coerced or cajoled to perform desired actions but they can not be owned in any sense. I can slaughter and eat animals but the act of eating their flesh does not mean that I own their flesh. For better or for worse, I have forcibly taken the flesh from the animal for my own use. By analogy, a thief can use property he or she has stolen but does not own that property.

I can not own the will, the spirit, the body, or the blood of another sentient being. Their will, their life force is their own. If it is not possible to own in any sense another sentient being, then it is not possible to sacrifice that being. The body and blood of that being are not mine to give.

In a human context, slavery is the name that we use for this kind of "ownership". I believe that the "owner"

never owned the "slave". He or she could force the slave to breed, labor, or even kill the slave but the slave's body and soul, though violated, remained their own. The owner could not legitimately sell or sacrifice the slave to the god of profit or to any other God. If what TC said and I write has some truth, then it must be considered that to offer animal sacrifice may open the door to a mentality which supports slavery.

Redefining Sacrifice:
Red Palm Oil and Sacred Journeys

S ummer 2001 — *About twenty drummers stood by the fire practicing before the night's ritual. I was demonstrating and talking about the rhythms. I like to drum and write but usually my own voice bores me. This was no exception so I yearned for the rite to begin.*

Suddenly a small frog jumped into the middle of the drummers. A few people tried to catch the frog without success. It was quick and unpredictable in its hopping. The drummer's feet and the fires hot ashes bracketed the frog's movements. The frog jumped toward me and I easily picked it up. I smiled. My ever hungry ego loves it when this kind of thing happens.

I carried the frog to the side of the field telling it that I was saving its life. I charged the frog to speak to its parents (Hecket) and ask that the night's rite be a success.

Someone yelled "Sacrifice" as I was walking with the frog.

Exactly correct, the frog was now charged to make a sacred pilgrimage. It was about the sacred and as such

was sacred.

Sacrifice is to "make sacred." A sentient being is supposedly made sacred by being sacrificed to a loa or some other spirit/God/dess. The sacrifice always involves the beings' suffering or death. These are the "givens" of sacrifice. But then, givens have a habit of changing; "what is" is often challenged by "what if." What if the death of the being were not a part of the sacrifice?

Ah! As an aside, there is a certain attractive drama in noting that as I was working on this section, a fly landed on the word "death" in the previous sentence, rolled over, and died. The insect loa seem to be reminding me to mention "that sometimes a sacrifice happens spontaneously without premeditation, like a deer hit by a car outside the ritual space during the rite, this has obviously been preordained" (Conversation 2003; Mishlen Linden). Honor, respect, and thanks to my small winged friend. May you find a glorious rebirth.

Without sacrifice, what would we, as practitioners, and the loa be left with? Can we create the kind of reciprocity with the loa engendered by sacrifice without taking sentient life? I believe so.

A powerful reciprocity can be achieved through the saving of life rather than its taking. A sentient being can be saved from some obvious peril and then charged to repay the assistance by telling its spiritual Grandfather and Grandmother (loa) two things; who

helped it and what the person helping it wants.

August 13, 1983 — Akoko came over to the loft. He brought a jar of Red Palm Oil and was near to raving about the power in the oil. He chewed on his beard, rolled his eyes, and contemplated the jar of oil he had carefully placed on the table. He told me to look at it with my spiritual eyes and I would be amazed. He said that the oil can be used instead of animal blood to feed the loa.

After he left I composed myself and studied the oil. Something that looked like smoke came from it. I am impressed and will give the oil a try.

The form and the appetites of the loa change. They change from country to country and region to region. The loa are not static, they are not tightly encased within the customs and appetites of a particular time and local. They live as we live and the essential quality of life is change. The loa do not wear the same clothing they wore thousands of years ago and they do not eat the same meals. I have found that Red Palm Oil nurtures and feeds the loa in the same manner as the flesh and blood of a sacrificed being. It is as if the Red Palm Oil is a special gift from the universe to voodooists who practice in the New Orleans style and possibly to practitioners in other styles. Its versatility is amazing in feeding the different loa.

Fair Trade Red Palm Oil can be purchased in African and Middle Eastern food stores or in spiritual botanicas. It combines the power of the color red with the sacredness of the tree. Red is the color of blood, meat, heat, and strength. Mange rouge or "red meal" is one name given to feedings of the loa that contain blood. Cultures such as the Tibetan, that no longer generally offer blood sacrifice, often color their offerings red. It is as if part of the nourishment found by the loa and spirits in blood derives from its very color. The tree is a link between heaven and earth. Its branches reach into the sky to pull down the powers of the heavens while its roots pierce the earth to drink from sacred underground waters. The Porteau Mitan that stands at the center of many a Voodoo Temple and through which the loa descend is often a living tree.

July, 1999 — I open the voodooists Heads to these (Insect) Loa. Potion to back of neck. The potion is composed of Red Palm Oil (as powerful as blood - contains no suffering of an animal), charged water, and sacred earths (Temple, Congo Square).

"When you begin to feel the insect loa coming on, take some of the food in the plate before you. The food is a red palm candy."

A sacrifice has at least two functions in New Orleans Voodoo. It acts to feed, to nurture the loa to whom the sacrifice is made and it acts to create reciprocity between the voodooist and the particular loa. Combining an offering of Red Palm Oil with the "Sacred Journey" of a being whose life is saved, these two functions can be satisfied without sacrifice and,

as an African acquaintance once said, "The chicken is much happier."

Western Medicine & Traditional Healing: The Guinea Pig and the Chicken

November 15, 1998 — I received a call from M. who is seeing a doctor about her painful and advancing arthritis. She told me that the serum recommended by her Dr. is recent and is made from chemicals harvested from rooster combs.

"Can you imagine how many roosters they have to kill to get that serum?"

"Lots" and then my voice dropped off.

To develop and exercise principals regarding animal sacrifice is perhaps most difficult in the area of medicine and healing. Animals are sacrificed and die so that sick human beings may recover and continue to live. The end is to save human life; the means involve the sacrificial death of animals. Here the basic questions are the same for both modern western medicine and for New Orleans Voodoo.

Is it permissible to sacrifice animals in order to save or attempt to save the lives of human beings? Ethically it makes no difference if the question is put to a medical doctor or to a voodoo priest. The proverbial chicken of voodoo and the guinea pig of science are both alike in sentience. They both actively seek happiness and the avoidance of suffering. Both seek to escape pain. The consistent application of principals and values is one defining characteristic of what we call fairness and justice. If there is an objection to animal sacrifice in New Orleans Voodoo, then this same objection must be applied to the sacrifice of animals by science.

The term "sacrifice" is used in western medical practice to describe the killing of an animal in order that its body may be studied, used in the preparation of medicines, or have its parts "harvested." In the science of medicine, animals are sacrificed and extracts from these animals are used to affect cures for the benefit of human beings. The healing of human beings through the means of western medicine frequently involves the sacrifice of animals.

It is not necessary to even broach the questionable area of animal testing or experimentation. One can be opposed to animal experimentation and still be agreeable to the use of animal's extracts for healing. Parts of animals are routinely harvested to create skin grafts and various serums. The heart of a baboon now beats in the chest of a human being.

In Voodoo, as in western medicine, the healing of human beings often involves the sacrifice of animals. The term "sacrifice" is used in the healing practices of New Orleans Voodoo to describe the killing of an animal for the loa and/or the use of its body in whole or in part for the preparation of medicines and spells. As in western medicine, parts of the body are often "harvested". Animal testing or experimentation is absent from Voodoo healing. The possible cruelties of this testing and experimentation are the sole property of western medicine.

Voodoo and western medicine both have certain rates of success and certain rates of failure in their standard treatments. To say that western medicine has a higher success rate and therefore it is legitimate to sacrifice animals for its cures simply side-steps the question. First, everyone does not agree that a higher success rate in the treatment of a human being justifies the sacrifice of an animal. Secondly, at what point does the success rate justify animal sacrifice? At 2%? 5%, 25%? There may be general agreement that higher success rates justify drastic means but there is little agreement on what constitutes a "high" success rate. Also, what if the animals sacrificed are of a "higher" order; for example dolphins and great apes? What if the animals are of an endangered species? Western medicines higher rate of success does not cap the question.

Another issue to be broached involves numbers; the number of lives sacrificed and the number of lives saved. A scientist can say, "If this pigeon dies, a compound found only in its pancreas can save the lives of many people." A Voodoo worker can declare, "If this pigeon dies, then all of these people can be saved from

the hurricane." Here we are talking about one or a few beings dying to save the lives of many beings.

The obverse must also be considered. Is it permissible to take the lives of many beings in order to save the life of one or a few beings? In particular, what if the many beings are animals and the one or few beings are human beings? To what extent does the good of one sentient being outweigh the good of another sentient being? If the death of two, three, four,...or a thousand "higher" or "lower" order animals were necessary to make the serum to save the life of one human being would this be acceptable? Does the good of a person outweigh the good of a mosquito, a chicken, of a goat, of an elephant, of a member of a severely endangered species, of another human being? We seem to make this decision every day when we eat meat. The issues are complex and deserve deep thought and prayer for insight.

Priest Oswan of the New Orleans Voodoo Spiritual Temple once told me that healing is needed "to the extent one is separate from God." I took his words to refer to a spiritual healing that may or may not affect the body. In the unique and powerful light of his words, it is possible to examine a healing of the body independently from a healing of the soul. A distinction can be made between what is healing to the body and what is healing to the soul, what makes the body well and what brings the soul closer to Spirit. There is a common assumption that what is good for the soul is good for the body and visa versa. This is true but only in some cases. The relationship can be good, bad, or simply neutral.

Actions of benefit to the body, actions that are healing to the body, can be poisonous in their effects on the soul. For example, a heart may be bought and transplanted from a healthy, poor woman to save the life of a sick, wealthy man. The body of the wealthy man would heal, but his soul would be poisoned by such an arrangement. The converse is also true. Actions of benefit to the soul, actions that are healing to the soul, can be poisonous in their effects on the body. A mother could sell her heart to provide food for her starving children. Here her soul sings in its journey to Spirit and her body suffers and dies. The use of multivitamins may be neutral; good for the body but does little to speed or hinder the soul in its flight toward a holy destination.

In a healing of the body, one can certainly be helped by the medical sacrifice of an animal. Chemicals react with chemicals in a given fashion no matter the ethics of their origin. An amazing array of bodily parts are interchangeable between human and other beings. The cornea of a medically sacrificed goat can restore sight to a human eye.

A cure involving the sacrifice of an animal in western medicine or traditional voodoo, may be beneficial to a healing of the body but pernicious in its effect on the soul. In thinking about sacrifice and healing, it is

important to know if the healing is for the body, the soul, or for both. In accepting or rejecting the use of animal sacrifice, I believe that it is important to apply the same criteria to both western and traditional healing practices. It is easy to see that animal sacrifice in medicine and traditional healing raises complicated issues. It does not seem to be consistent to oppose animal sacrifice in Voodoo's traditional medicine and condone its use in the western science of medicine.

A Fish Story, 1984

I stopped before a fish vendor while walking down one of the small, alley like streets in China Town. He held out a large catfish for my scrutiny. The elderly man's wispy white beard hung barely visible before his black clothing. His kind eyes were slightly down cast and his mouth carried a little smile that radiated an evident pride in his catch. The long, thin mouth hairs of the catfish trembled. The fish's eyes bulged with fear. Its mouth opened and closed in a vain search for water and the relief of its suffering. "You like? You like?" said the man. I don't know what words swam and tumbled behind the fish's thick lips.

I bowed slightly, a bit sadly, to the vast richness of life and its awe full capacity to elude easy answers.

1. "Is it necessary to sacrifice animals in order to conduct an initiation or other ceremony to the loa?"

2. "Will I participate in ceremonies in which animals are sacrificed?"
3. "Will I myself sacrifice animals?"

I have attempted to provide a firmer ground for answering these three questions. My position is that there is no right or wrong to this. Only the careful machinations of spiritual cause and effect. Hold another sentient being in your hands. Its life is now literally in your hands as your life is just as literally in your own hands. Choice stands at the wheel in navigating this river of the soul. There is no condemnation or commendation, only an ever-present responsibility that is built into the very fabric of the universe. Think deeply. We can choose our actions, there is no choose involved in the consequences that they, by their nature, call forth.

A Very Personal Aside on Animal Sacrifice

I have joined New Orleans Voodoo, the faith of my land and city, to Buddhism. This is similar to what many of the people of Burma, Thailand, etc. have done with the faiths of their lands and cities for centuries. The words to follow are not meant to invoke any sense of "right" or "wrong." I wish to simply point out a way I have found that works for me and allows me to cause the least amount of harm possible.

In light of my blending of New Orleans Voodoo and Tibetan Buddhism, it would be nonsensical to offer animal sacrifice when doing a healing of the soul or mind stream. The Tibetan Tantrics speak of a mysterious force that they call "karma." To the best of my understanding, karma is like spiritual cause and effect in that you get back what you habitually give. If I cause suffering, then I receive suffering in return and animal sacrifice certainly causes some level of suffering in the being that is sacrificed. The use of a scapegoat would also be ineffective. To transfer my problems to another sentient being would cause that being suffering and open me up to karmic suffering. Karma is not so much "Do unto others as you would have them do

unto you" as "As you do unto others so shall be done unto you."

The Tibetan Tantrics also speak of reincarnation; we are migratory beings moving from one life to the next. Reincarnation holds that some subtle sense of who we are travels through these lifetimes. Moreover, the karma we accumulate affects these future incarnations. The combination of karma and reincarnation presents a powerful incentive for me to look deeply into my actions and their consequences. Even if I manage to avoid consequences in this life, they may very well be waiting for me in my next incarnation.

Given karma and reincarnation, I would be extremely wary of offering animal sacrifice to heal my body. To cure myself by taking life could create the seeds for a karmic situation worse than the present disease. Even if the disease were cured, the taking of the life could engender more future suffering on my part than the threatening disease could cause now.

Would I be more amenable to sacrificing an animal to save a friends life than to save my own life? The impulse of honor is to put the good of another above your own good. In combat, it might mean taking a blow meant for another. The karma involved in animal sacrifice is appreciable. To sacrifice a chicken to save a sick friend means that I would take the painful karma from that act upon myself. This is a difficult question at best. I do not know the answer. I do know that I would exhaust all other avenues before considering animal sacrifice. Wisdom has been called "the knowledge of necessity." I would not causally bring possible harm to myself; I would want to act wisely. I have found that with the use of Fair Trade Red Palm Oil instead of sacrifice, it may not be necessary for a practitioner to take on such a terrible load.

If karma and reincarnation or something like them is real, then to offer animal sacrifice may be to put oneself at risk not only in this life but also in future lives. It is not a matter of right or wrong or of good or bad. It is simply a matter of happiness and suffering. Some events in one's life tend to engender suffering and some events tend to engender happiness. Taking life usually engenders suffering and preserving life usually engenders happiness and pleasure. The karma from these acts pursues us through our future lifetimes.

Reincarnation also brings up two other considerations. The first is that we are human now and have been an animal before and will be a thousand different things in a thousand different moments of time. So in animal sacrifice I would not simply be killing an animal, I would be killing a sentient being that may have been human like me.

The second and most important consideration is a result of the infinite number of incarnations we experience. Given an infinite number of incarnations, the animal I would be sacrificing now had a special relationship to me at some point. The animal has been my mother or my father, my wife/husband or best

friend. The animal, in that past incarnation, loved and protected me. As Mother or Father it kept me from harm. To cause suffering to a being that at one time has benefited me so much is an awful thing, a thing without honor.

To say that the loa "Ogun wields the knife, not I" does not quite measure up. If this animal was my mother, my father, or my wife/husband at a different time, I am under a strong emotional and intellectual mandate to stop Ogun or any spirit or loa or human, that wields that knife. If my mother, wife, or friend were threatened by any person, spirit, or loa, I would act to help them, not sit by passively.

Even if it is true that it is Ogun who wields the knife and not I, there are still consequences I must face. I have entered into a relationship with Ogun. I have joined with him in these actions. I am allowing him to use my hand, my arm knowing full well that he will deliver a killing blow. The relationship I have entered into with Ogun joins us and will act as a weight around my neck. When this Ogun sinks under the weight of his karma, he will pull me down to the same fate. Also, if I have a love for the loa, of which Ogun is one, I would not want to put him or any of the other loa in such a harmful karmic situation.

I found that Red Palm Oil has proven to be every bit as effective for me in my practice as the life and blood of animals. This is a happy discovery. I would recommend that the practitioner reader try Fair Trade

Red Palm Oil. If it works for you as it does for me, maybe there will be a bit less suffering in the world. Maybe.

Addendum I

Protocols of Sacred Giving

	GIFT	PRESENT	OFFERING	SACRIFICE*
FORM consists of . .	Usually an object	An object, action, or process	An object, action, or process. Does not involve the suffering of what is offered.	The life of or flesh or blood or organs from a living being
FUNCTION used to . .	Giving only. No expected benefits.	Giving only. No expected benefits.	Giving with an expectation of benefit.	CAN BE Giving only thus involving no expected benefits. (Gift, Present) OR Giving with an expectation of benefit (Sacrifice).

* A sacrifice given with no expected benefit can be referred to as "a gift of a sacrifice" or "a present of a sacrifice."
For example, "I made a gift of a sacrifice to Papa Legba" or "A present of a sacrifice can be made to Papa Legba".

A sacrifice given with expectation of benefit can be referred to simply as a "sacrifice".

A sacrifice cannot be an offering. An offering as defined does not include the death or suffering of a living being. In this writing I have avoided the use of the verb "offer" to avoid confusion.

Gifts, Presents, and Offerings to the Loa and Spirits of New Orleans Voodoo: An Overview

The What and Why of Sacred Giving

As an overall rule, there is often a similarity between the qualities of "what" is given and the reason or "why" it is given. Like engenders like. One can give white rice to a loa in order to receive the benefits of peace, not gunpowder. A weapon is given to strike down an enemy, not Florida Water. Silk can be given to receive the virtue of gentleness, not iron. Cool water is given to gain a cool head, not fire.

Gifts and presents add to the power of the loa and spirits to whom they are given. Offerings acknowledge and celebrate that power. Remember to set boundaries as to what you will give in ritual. Stretch your boundaries in a manner that makes you both more inclusive and more focused on what you now perceive as the greatest good. You are of spirit no less than the loa or other deities, ancestors such as Babatunde Olatunji, Mr. Crowley, and Sun Ra understood this well.

General Sacred Giving

Rum and tobacco are given in New Orleans Voodoo during general rites conducted to give honor and respect to all of the loa during a single ritual. The more time and attention put into preparation, the more pleasing the giving will be to the loa. The time and attention are in themselves powerful to give (present) to the loa. In general, it is not so much crucial what is given as the spirit in which it is shared. If the giving is not to the loa's liking but was offered with respect, it is common for the loa to come in dreams or in a more direct manner and declare his or her desires.

Specific Sacred Giving

The loa are individuals with specific tastes and as such they want specific types of gifts, presents, or offerings. If you are not sure or feel an uneasiness about something specifically given, then simply ask the loa what he or she wants. The loa are close, they will reply. A table of possible and I would emphasize possible, gifts/presents/offerings follows. Be respectful and creative in your choices and you will travel on a firm road.

The following table contains a list of several of the loa local to New Orleans Voodoo and a few loa served in wider geographical areas. It provides foods, objects and actions I have found to their liking. The foods, objects and

actions have the necessary qualities to please and strengthen these loa.

Some of these loa were born and grew here and are specific to the land and waters of New Orleans. If they speak to you, it may be that you presently live here or have lived here in the past of this life or of another life. If they seem simply peculiar and they do not speak to you, then may their grace inspire you to look for the loa and spirits of the land that you inhabit. The soil that supports you this moment is every bit as sacred as the soil of Congo Square.

This table does differ from the table I created for the New Orleans Voodoo Tarot. The additional years of practice have sharpened my appreciation of New Orleans Voodoo's loa. It is good to remember that new loa are arising all of the time and no table is definitive.

The organization follows the Hebraic glyph of the Tree of Life as interpreted by the Golden Dawn. This is simply for convenience and the reader need know nothing about this Tree to use the list. If other systems of organization are more useful, by all means, utilize them.

Gifts, Presents, and Offerings to the Loa and Spirits of New Orleans Voodoo

1. Kether

Da

"Da" means movement (serpent as pure movement) and is a root of names such as Damballa Wedo and Ayida Wedo.

KEY ASSOCIATION: All movement. Any movement between the visible and the invisible worlds.

SOLID OBJECT: Glass (glass is always flowing), a crown.

LIQUID: Clear water.

MINERAL: Quicksilver, metaphoric rocks - shaped by heat and pressure, meteorite.

TREE/FLOWER: Plant morning glory - a quick growing plant. Plant a calabash tree.

FOOD (Fruit, Vegetable, Grain): Gourd - the sound of a shaken gourd (rattle) can be used to move between the worlds. Squash - resembles a gourd.

ACTIONS: Any movement of the body.
CELEBRATION: St. John's Eve

2. Chokmah
Grand Zombi / Danny Boy

This is the great Temple Snake. The New Orleans Voodoo use of "zombie" is not meant to be confused with the Haitian use of the word. The serpent spirits of New Orleans Voodoo walk a path similar to Damballa Wedo and Ayida Wedo. The beloved Temple Snake of John T. Martin of the Historic Voodoo Museum carried the name Zombi.

KEY ASSOCIATION: The essence of all Temple Snakes, good council.

SOLID OBJECT: Mardi Gras Beads, necklaces, strings of beads, lightning, shed skin of a snake.

LIQUID: Fresh water.

MINERAL: Snake Skin Agate.

FOOD (Fruit/Vegetable/Grain): Your own favorite foods. The Grand Zombi is one of the most inclusive of spirits.

ACTIONS: Deep meditation, stillness, heat, warmth (rub your hands together).

CELEBRATION: Saint Patrick's Day.

Marassa

The Marassa are the Divine Twins. They govern both duality and its reconciliation.

KEY ASSOCIATION: Balance, Ibeji, twins, twin children, child like behaviors, gateway, 2X.

SOLID OBJECT: Any doubled object.

LIQUID: A sweet drink, cola.

FOOD (Fruit, Vegetable, Grain): Candy, a soft, sweet fruit or vegetable.

MINERAL: A shiny stone, magnetic load stones that pull together.

TREE/FLOWER: Plant a dicot plant, i.e. having two embryonic leaves such as a Magnolia, any bright plant.

ACTIONS: Any childlike action.

CELEBRATION: Christmas.

3. Binah
Manman Bridgette

An honored, great judge. She has Baron Samedi as her husband.

KEY ASSOCIATION: Judgment both fair and merciful of the living and the dead. She loves to care for aborted

fetuses...they are as flowers in her garden.

SOLID OBJECT: Rocks piled, red bricks piled (rocks are not always easy to find in new Orleans).

LIQUID: A dark rum.

FOOD (Fruit, Vegetable, Grain): Pink and white Birthday cake.

MINERAL: Grave yard dust.

TREE/FLOWER: Cyprus, nettle.

ACTIONS: Any decision or judgment come to by carefully weighing merit. Building a fence, making a pile of rocks.

CELEBRATION: May 5th.

4. Chesed

Mama Waters

Mama Waters is the great mother of all waters, from the waters of birth to the waters used to wash a fresh corpse. The Marassa are her twin children.

KEY ASSOCIATION: Water as the planets life blood.

SOLID OBJECT: Any waters; in particularly those that proceed birth and...

LIQUID: Salt water.

FOOD (Fruit, Vegetable, Grain): Any fruit containing plentiful liquids, Sea Weed.

MINERAL: Calcium carbonate (sea shells are composed of this).

FLOWER: Water a plant.

TREE: Water a tree.

ACTIONS: Bathing as a purification, drinking water.

CELEBRATION: Thanksgiving as the end of hurricane season.

Black Hawk

A great chief and protector of the Indian Nation.

KEY ASSOCIATION: Protection, dignity under duress, Watcher on the Wall.

SOLID OBJECT: Red candles, red cloth, peace pipe, tomahawk (cutting through obstacles), spear (especially in dancing and for reaching a distant goal), feathers.

LIQUID: Red or golden; nonalcoholic, clear water.

FOOD (Fruit, Vegetable, Grain): Maize, corn.

MINERAL: Fertile soil.

ACTIONS: Slow dignified dance.

CELEBRATION: December, usually the 17th.

Gros Bon Ange

The Gros Bon Ange is the Big or Fat Good Angel. The personality of this Angel can be identified with universal love.

KEY ASSOCIATION: Love as expansion, any expansion, angel.

SOLID OBJECT: Any figure of a beneficent angel.

LIQUID: Mixture of liquid elements such as a perfume.

MINERAL: A rock that brings together different materials.

TREE/FLOWER: Give tree or flower seeds to the earth.

FOOD (Fruit, Vegetable, Grain): Give the seeds of fruit or vegetable to the earth. Give a meal that combines two or more foods.

ACTIONS: An outward breath, looking at stars in the night sky, becoming the power of conjure itself.

CELEBRATION: Any celebration of uniting or joining, a marriage of some kind.

5. Geburah

Mademoiselle Katrina

The hurricane that struck New Orleans and the Gulf Coast. This spirit walks a path similar to that of Oya.

KEY ASSOCIATION: A swift, violent event that changes all after its occurrence. One moment in which all futures are changed, massive wind.

SOLID OBJECT: Broken glass, damaged materials.

LIQUID: Rain, Storm water.

FOOD (Fruit, Vegetable, Grain): Give canned foods (survived the storm).

MINERAL: Mud

TREE/FLOWER: Any broken wood.

ACTIONS: A whirling dance.

CELEBRATION: August 29th

Joe Fer

Iron Joe. Walks a road similar to that of the Oguns.

KEY ASSOCIATION: Strong man, superhuman strength and stamina.

SOLID OBJECT: Any object made of iron, old iron nails, anvil.

LIQUID: High proof alcohol.

FOOD (Fruit, Vegetable, Grain): Spicy foods.

MINERAL: Iron.

TREE/FLOWER: Ironwood.

ACTIONS: Dance with moves like beating on an anvil, strenuous physical activity.

CELEBRATION: Mardi Gras.

Annie Christmas

In folklore, a woman who worked the docks as everything from a steamboat captain to a stevedore to the owner of a bordello. Possessed of superhuman strength and stamina.

KEY ASSOCIATION: Strong Woman.

SOLID OBJECT: Machete (especially for dance), silver, silver coins.

LIQUID: High proof alcohol.

FOOD (Fruit, Vegetable, Grain): Spicy foods.

MINERAL: Diamond, stones with sparkle, rhinestones.

TREE/FLOWER: Plant a Begonia (Big, red flowers).

ACTIONS: Dance with machete, gambling, gaiety, actions of hard work.

CELEBRATION: Mardi Gras (abandon).

6. Tiphereth
Blanc Dan-i

White Snake, Male or Female or both, walks a path similar to that of Oba Tala.

KEY ASSOCIATION: Balance, patience, kindness, a wise elder, albino African American.

SOLID OBJECT: Clean, white clothing; white pearls or beads.

LIQUID: Clear water.

MINERAL: Smooth, white stone.

TREE/FLOWER: Plant a magnolia.

FOODS (Fruit, Vegetable, Grain): White rice.

ACTIONS: Active silence, contemplation.

CELEBRATION: Easter, the risen Christ.

Papa Labat/Papa Legba/Papa La Bas

The gate opener between the Visible and Invisible Worlds. An old man who walks with a limp.

KEY ASSOCIATIONS: Opener of the gate, gatekeeper.

SOLID OBJECT: Any gate, toy or real, a cane, pipe tobacco.

LIQUID: Rum.

TREE/FLOWER: Plant a tall growing tree.

FOODS (Fruit, Vegetable, Grain): Any fruit, vegetable, or grain that grows from the earth into the sky.

ACTIONS: Allowing passage through or around some obstacle, story telling.

Ti Bon Ange

The small, good angel. Associated with the will of the worker.

KEY ASSOCIATION: Will, individual choice.

OBJECT: Any symbol or record of personal success.

LIQUID: Distilled water.

MINERAL: Crystal with a single point.

TREE/FLOWER: Plant a monocot plant, i.e. having one embryonic leaf such as grass.

FOODS (Fruit, Vegetable, Grain): Give a meal in which one food only is eaten.

ACTIONS: The in breath.

CELEBRATION: Individual birth.

7. Netzach
Marie Laveau

The great priestess of New Orleans Voodoo. Renowned leader of rites on Congo Square.

KEY ASSOCIATION: The Priestess, the dancer.

SOLID OBJECT: An honored chair dedicated to her use.

LIQUID: A perfume.

MINERAL: Gold.

TREE/FLOWER: Plant a rose bush.

FOOD (Fruit, Vegetable, Grain): Give a grand meal.

ACTIONS: A recitation of her children's names, light a candle for her in a Roman Catholic Church, dance.

CELEBRATION: St. John's Eve, Birth and Death date: September 10, 1801 - June 15,1881 (the years continue to be debated), marriage to Jacques Paris on August 4th, 1819.

Queen Margaret

Much honored practitioner of New Orleans Voodoo. She passed into the invisible World shortly after Hurricane Katrina.

KEY ASSOCIATION: An Elder Priestess with dignified bearing. Knowledge through study and practice. Direct communication with the loa/spirits. Giving, beneficence, generosity.

SOLID OBJECT: A book, tignon, white beads, gold rimmed glasses, asson.

LIQUID: A subtle perfume.

MINERAL: Turquoise.

TREE/FLOWER: Plant a rose.

FOOD (Fruit, Vegetable, Grain): Give brown rice.

ACTIONS: The demeanor of an elder priestess competently residing over a ceremony.

CELEBRATION: St John's Eve.

Priestess Rose Yaffa Frank

Yoruba and Voodoo Priestess.

KEY ASSOCIATION: Deep study of metaphysics.

SOLID OBJECT: Mirror, sea glass, cooking pot.

LIQUID: Sea water and by extension salt water.

MINERAL: Turquoise, rhodochrosite.

TREE/FLOWER: Gladiola.

FOOD (Fruit, Vegetable, Grain): Rice.

ACTIONS: Dance, stirring the pot.

CELEBRATION: St. John's Eve, All Saints Day

8. Hod
Dr. John Montanee

The spirit and loa of male voodoo practitioners. A drummer and spiritual doctor.

KEY ASSOCIATION: The drummer, the spiritual doctor, priest.

SOLID OBJECT: A drum, percussion instrument, herbs.

LIQUID: Any medicinal liquid, i.e. camphor.

MINERAL: Any mineral that can be taken medicinally.

TREE/FLOWER: Plant any tree or flower used medicinally.

FOOD (Fruit, Vegetable, Grain): Medicinal use of fruit, vegetable, or grain.

ACTIONS: Drumming, spiritual healing.

CELEBRATION: Any celebration of drummers or drums, St. John's Eve, Deathdate: August 23rd, 1885.

Priest Oswan Chamani

Along with Priestess Miriam, founder of the New Orleans Voodoo Spiritual Temple.

KEY ASSOCIATION: Priest, healer, scholar, diviner, Ibo lele, wise council.

SOLID OBJECT: Herbs in their medicinal applications.

LIQUID: Mango juice, Tacka Vodka (half beer and half vodka) chased with beer.

MINERAL: Jasper, Blood stone, amethyst, quartz crystal.

TREE/FLOWER: Mango tree.

FOOD (Fruit, Vegetable, Grain): Jamaican Roti.

ACTIONS: The movements of a scholar and a priest, writing with a "proper" pencil.

CELEBRATION: March 6th. Passing into the arms of the ancestors.

Charles Massicott Gandolfo (preferred)/ Voodoo Charlie / Dr. Charlie

Curator and founder of the New Orleans Historic Voodoo Museum.

KEY ASSOCIATION: Deep study and knowledge of New Orleans Voodoo, joie de vivre, artist, love of Creole culture.

SOLID OBJECT: Hat, museum, any collection, Mardi Gras beads.

LIQUID: Rum, beer.

MINERAL: Agate.

TREE/FLOWER: Magnolia.

FOOD (Fruit, Vegetable, Grain): Creole foods, Tobassco sauce.

ACTIONS: Collecting and examining spiritual objects, studying Louisiana history.

CELEBRATION: Mardi Gras Day, the day he passed into the arms of the ancestors.

King Joshua Frank

Grande Voodooist, tour guide for the New Orleans Historic Voodoo Museum.

KEY ASSOCIATION: Voodoo King of New Orleans.

SOLID OBJECT: A cane.

LIQUID: Rum.

TREE/FLOWER: Cotton, tobacco plant.

FOOD (Fruit, Vegetable, Grain): Southern Soul Food, yams especially.

ACTIONS: Hollering, calling the spirits, singing in Creole.

CELEBRATION: St. John's Eve.

9. Yesod
Loup Garou

Swamp beasts, human and beast combined, wolf-like creature.

KEY ASSOCIATION: Mysterie and danger, can be sent on expeditions to help or harm.

SOLID OBJECT: Dolls, small plastic babies (enslaved female Africans were told by the planters they would turn into wolves if they did not bear babies).

LIQUID: Swamp water, brackish water.

FOOD (Fruit, Vegetable, Grain): Plantain brushed with Red Palm Oil.

MINERAL: Coal (carbon).

TREE/FLOWER: Cyprus, Spanish moss.

ACTIONS: Animal like movements

10. Malkuth
Congo Square

A site across from Rampart Street where enslaved Africans, Native Americans, and Poor Whites would set up a market, sing, dance, and play music. The dances are associated with Marie Laveau and Dr. John Montanee during mid eighteen hundreds.

KEY ASSOCIATION: Material manifestation of movement, the living focus of New Orleans Voodoo.

SOLID OBJECT: Veve or drawing of the square.

LIQUID: Water from Congo Square.

FOOD (Fruit, Vegetable, Grain): The fruit Plantain. Grow a fruit or vegetable in earth from Congo Square.

MINERAL: Stones or earth from Congo Square.

TREE/FLOWER: Plant a flower or tree in the soil from Congo Square.

ACTIONS: A vender's dance.

CELEBRATION: Any market, Sunday, St. John's Eve (Congo Square and Bayou St. John).

The la Flambeau aspects of the above loa/spirits are fiery in nature. Add hot sauce to foods and liquids.

Veve of New Orleans
by Mishlen Linden

Other Publications by

BLACK MOON PUBLISHING

Typhonian Teratomas
The Shadows of the Abyss by Mishlen Linden

The Faces of Babalon
A Compilation of Women's Voices by Mishlen Linden,
Linda Falorio, Soror Chen, Nema and Raven Greywalker

Waters of Return
The Aeonic Flow of Voudoo by Louis Martinié

A Priest's Head, A Drummer's Hands
New Orleans Voodoo Order of Service by Louis Martinié

Feather & Firesnake : The Maat of Kundalini
by Nema

The Priesthood
Parameters and Responsibilities by Nema

Maatian Meditations and Considerations
A Continuation of Past Writings on "She Who Moves"
by Nema

Wings of Rapture
by Nema

Enochian Temples
by Benjamin Rowe

The Book of the Seniors
by Benjamin Rowe

The 91 Parts of the Earth
by Benjamin Rowe

BLACKMOONPUBLISHING.COM

About the Book

This text is important to anyone who follows a set of religious practices that may include sacrifice, particularly the sacrifice of animals. Its goal is to create a framework that makes it possible for the practitioner to approach the issue of animal sacrifice on the secure footing of systematic thought coupled with deep feeling; hopefully avoiding the slippery and sensationalistic aversion or attraction too often associated with the subject. Both the pros and cons of animal sacrifice are examined and the author proposes alternatives to sacrifice of sentient beings.

"Think; deeply contemplate actions and their alternatives and the fruit that they bear. Choose freely and wisely. Choice stands at the wheel in navigating this river of the soul. There is no condemnation or commendation, only an ever-present responsibility that is built into the very fabric of the universe. We can choose in our actions; there is no choice involved in the consequences that they, by their nature, call forth."

About the Author

Dr. Louie Martinié is a drummer, an elder, and a spiritual doctor in service to the New Orleans Voodoo Spiritual Temple for over 20 years. He is the Content Editor for Black Moon Publishing and his writings include co-authorship of the *New Orleans Voodoo Tarot* (Destiny) and *A Priest's Head, A Drummer's Hands* (Black Moon Publishing).

His current work includes ritual and research focused on bringing Honor and Respect to John Montanee, the original Dr. John who drummed with Marie Laveau. He is a member of Bate Cabal and an honorary member of the Louisiana Legislature. Blanc Dan-i is the Master of his Head; the Marassa sing within his heart.

Dr. Louie Martinié

www.ingramcontent.com/pod-product-compliance
Lightning Source LLC
Chambersburg PA
CBHW030855090426
42737CB00009B/1239